新月集

· THE CRESCENT MOON ·

（英汉对照）

（印）泰戈尔 著

郑振铎 译

机械工业出版社
CHINA MACHINE PRESS

《新月集》是泰戈尔的代表作之一，具有很大的影响，在世界各地被译为多种文字版本，是最早被译为中文版本的泰戈尔作品之一。在诗中，诗人生动地描绘了儿童们的游戏，巧妙地表现了孩子们的心理，以及他们活泼的想象。它特殊隽永的艺术魅力把我们带到了一个纯洁美丽的儿童世界，勾起了我们对于童年生活的美好回忆和向往。

图书在版编目（CIP）数据

新月集：英汉对照 /（印）泰戈尔著；郑振铎译 . —北京：机械工业出版社，2017.12

（读经典　学英文）

ISBN 978-7-111-58948-8

Ⅰ . ①新… Ⅱ . ①泰… ②郑… Ⅲ . ①英语—汉语—对照读物 ②诗集—印度—现代 Ⅳ . ① H319.4 : I

中国版本图书馆 CIP 数据核字（2018）第 008301 号

机械工业出版社（北京市百万庄大街 22 号 邮政编码 100037）
策划编辑：尹小云 责任编辑：尹小云
版式设计：墨格文慧 责任印制：孙　炜
保定市中画美凯印刷有限公司印刷

2018 年 2 月第 1 版第 1 次印刷
148mm×210mm · 5.375 印张 · 1 插页 · 73 千字
0 001—5 000 册
标准书号：ISBN 978-7-111-58948-8
定价：29.80 元

关 于 作 者

罗宾德拉纳特·泰戈尔（Rabindranath Tagore, 1861—1941）是一位享誉世界的印度诗人、小说家、艺术家、思想家与社会活动家，是第一位获得诺贝尔文学奖的亚洲人。他一生写了50多部诗集，被称为"诗圣"。

泰戈尔出生在印度一个富有哲学与文学修养的贵族家庭，8岁就开始写诗，13岁便能对长诗与颂歌体诗进行创作，展现出非凡的文学天赋。1913年，他因自译的英文版《吉檀迦利》荣获诺贝尔文学奖，自此跻身于世界文坛。

泰戈尔的作品具有极高的历史、艺术价值，深受民众喜爱。其主要诗作有不少被世人熟知，如《新月集》《吉檀迦利》《飞鸟集》《采果集》《园丁集》等。

泰戈尔是一位对整个世界都有着巨大影响的作家，除了诸多诗集外，还创作了12部中长篇小说，100多部短篇小说，20多部剧本以及大量的文学、哲学、政治论著，并在70岁高龄时开始学习绘画，创作出了1 500多幅极为珍贵的图画。此外，他还创作了不计其数的各类歌曲。其作品内容几乎无所不包。

　　泰戈尔的著作早在 1915 年便被介绍到了中国，他影响了一批中国最有才华的诗人与作家。其中郭沫若、冰心等所受到的影响最深，郭沫若就曾称自己文学生涯的第一阶段是"泰戈尔式"的。

关 于 作 品

　　《新月集》创作于 1903 年，是泰戈尔的代表作之一。该诗集以描绘孩子们的游戏和童趣的方式巧妙地把孩子们的纯洁心理与奇特活泼的思维方式展现给了世人。泰戈尔在诗集中想要讴歌的便是人的一生中最为宝贵的心性：童真。

　　除了描绘孩童的纯真，该诗集还极力赞美母爱。正如现实中没有母爱的孩子不可能体会到幸福是什么一样，他深谙个中哲理，在作品中把这两种截然不同却息息相关的事物融合到了一起，共同地给予了赞颂。正是如此，才使诗的本身深具思想哲理，且使诗中所描绘的孩子们更加有血有肉、感情丰富。诗集问世之后，泰戈尔还因此被誉为"儿童诗人"。

　　"如果人们知道了我的国王的宫殿在哪里，它就会消失在空气中的。

　　"墙壁是白色的银，屋顶是耀眼的黄金。

　　"皇后住在有七个庭院的宫苑里；她戴的一串珠宝，值整整七个王国的全部财富。

　　"不过，让我悄悄地告诉你，妈妈，我的国王的宫殿究竟在哪里。

　　"它就在我们阳台的角上，在那栽着杜尔茜花的花盆放着

新月集

The Crescent Moon

的地方。"

这是多么可爱的孩童心理呀！天真的、纯洁的、无瑕的、带着孩子喜爱玩闹的恶作剧的诗句，《新月集》就是这么充满着童真。

每一首诗都仿佛有着不可抗拒的魔力，把我们从罪恶的、贪婪的、黑暗的世道之中牵引到一个纯洁而天真的孩童世界，不仅勾起了我们对童年纯粹而美好生活的回忆，还剪去了在现实困境里苦苦挣扎着的这些人们心中阴暗的一隅，净化心灵、陶冶性情。

关 于 译 者

郑振铎（1898—1958），著名文学家、作家、翻译家和文物考古学家，同时也是我国新文化和新文学运动的倡导者。

新中国成立以后，郑振铎历任中央人民政府文化部文物事业管理局局长、中国科学院考古研究所所长及文学研究所所长、文化部副部长、国务院科学规划委员会委员、中国科学院哲学社会科学部委员、中国民间文艺研究理事会副主席等职。

他的主要著作有《插图本中国文学史》《中国俗文学史》《中国文学研究》《俄国文学史略》《近百年古城古墓发掘史》等，译著有《新月集》《飞鸟集》等，另有《郑振铎文集》。郑振铎的一生都投身于翻译工作，不仅著述丰富，而且他发表的大量译作、译论在中国翻译史上也占有极为重要的地位，为我国的文学与翻译领域做出了巨大贡献。

他在 1922 年和 1923 年两年间翻译出版了泰戈尔的《飞鸟集》与《新月集》，从此便开始系统地、大量地对泰戈尔的诗歌进行翻译。冰心在看了郑振铎所译的《飞鸟集》之后，做出

新月集

The Crescent Moon

的评价是："觉得那小诗非常自由，就学了那种自由的写法，随时把自己的感想和回忆，三言两语写下来。"这些译作对中国当时的文坛产生了直接影响，而且对促进中国新文学与外国文学的交流也起到了非常重要的作用。

因郑振铎主要翻译的是泰戈尔的诗歌及印度古代的寓言，印度著名学者海曼歌·比斯瓦斯对他在印度文化方面的翻译贡献给予了很高的评价。在他去世后，海曼歌·比斯瓦斯在1958年《悼念郑振铎》一文中写道："他可能是第一个把印度古典文学和现代文学介绍给中国读者的人，他同样是当前中印文化交流的先驱。"

目录
CONTENTS

新月集

The Crescent Moon

I shall become a delicate draught of air and caress you; and I shall be ripples in the water when you bathe, and kiss you and kiss you again.

我要变成一股清风抚摸着你；我要变成水的涟漪，当你浴时，把你吻了又吻。

The Home

I paced alone on the road across the field while the sunset was hiding its last gold like a miser.

The daylight sank deeper and deeper into the darkness, and the widowed land, whose harvest had been reaped, lay silent.

Suddenly a boy's shrill voice rose into the sky. He traversed the dark unseen, leaving the track of his song across the hush of the evening.

His village home lay there at the end of the waste land, beyond the sugar-cane field, hidden among the shadows of the banana and the slender areca palm, the cocoa-nut and the dark green jack-fruit trees.

I stopped for a moment in my lonely way

家 庭

我独自在横跨过田地的路上走着。夕阳像一个守财奴似的，正藏起它最后的金子。

白昼更加深沉地没入黑暗之中。那已经收割了的孤寂的田地，默默地躺在那里。

天空里突然升起了一个男孩子的尖锐的歌声。他穿过看不见的黑暗，留下他的歌声的辙痕跨过黄昏的静谧。

他的乡村的家坐落在荒凉的土地的边上，在甘蔗田的后面，躲藏在香蕉树、瘦长的槟榔树、椰子树和深绿色的贾克果树的阴影里。

我在星光下独自走着的路上停留了一会儿。我

under the starlight, and saw spread before me the darkened earth surrounding with her arms countless homes furnished with cradles and beds, mothers' hearts and evening lamps, and young lives glad with a gladness that knows nothing of its value for the world.

看见黑沉沉的大地展开在我的面前，用她的手臂拥抱着无量数的家庭。在那些家庭里有着摇篮和床铺，母亲们的心和夜晚的灯，还有年轻轻的生命。他们满心欢乐，却浑然不知这样的欢乐对于世界的价值。

On the Seashore

On the seashore of endless worlds children meet.

The infinite sky is motionless overhead and the restless water is boisterous. On the seashore of endless worlds the children meet with shouts and dances.

They build their houses with sand, and they play with empty shells. With withered leaves they weave their boats and smilingly float them on the vast deep. Children have their play on the seashore of worlds.

They know not how to swim; they know not how to cast nets. Pearl-fishers dive for pearls, merchants sail in their ships, while children gather pebbles and scatter them again. They seek not for hidden treasures; they know not how to cast nets.

海　边

孩子们会集在无边无际的世界的海边。

无限的天穹静止地临于头上，不息的海水在足下汹涌。孩子们会集在无边无际的世界的海边，叫着，跳着。

他们拿沙来建筑房屋，拿空贝壳来做游戏。他们把落叶编成了船，笑嘻嘻地把它们放到大海上。孩子们在世界的海边，做他们的游戏。

他们不知道怎样泅水，他们不知道怎样撒网。采珠的人为了珠潜水，商人在他们的船上航行，孩子们却只把小圆石聚了又散。他们不搜求宝藏；他们不知道怎样撒网。

The sea surges up with laughter, and pale gleams the smile of the sea-beach. Death-dealing waves sing meaningless ballads to the children, even like a mother while rocking her baby's cradle. The sea plays with children, and pale gleams the smile of the sea-beach.

On the seashore of endless worlds children meet. Tempest roams in the pathless sky, ships are wrecked in the trackless water, death is abroad and children play. On the seashore of endless worlds is the great meeting of children.

大海哗笑着涌起波浪，而海滩的微笑荡漾着淡淡的光芒。致人死命的波涛，对着孩子们唱无意义的歌曲，就像一个母亲在摇动她孩子的摇篮时一样。大海和孩子们一同游戏，而海滩的微笑荡漾着淡淡的光芒。

孩子们会集在无边无际的世界的海边。狂风暴雨飘游在无辙迹的天空上，航船沉碎在无辙迹的海水里，死正在外面活动，孩子们却在游戏。在无边无际的世界的海边，孩子们大会集着。

The Source

The sleep that flits on baby's eyes—does anybody know from where it comes? Yes, there is a rumour that it has its dwelling where, in the fairy village among shadows of the forest dimly lit with glow-worms, there hang two shy buds of enchantment. From there it comes to kiss baby's eyes.

The smile that flickers on baby's lips when he sleeps—does anybody know where it was born? Yes, there is a rumour that a young pale beam of a crescent moon touched the edge of a vanishing autumn cloud, and there the smile was first born in the dream of a dew-washed morning—the smile that flickers on baby's lips when he sleeps.

The sweet, soft freshness that blooms on baby's limbs—does anybody know where it was hidden so long? Yes, when the mother was a young girl it lay pervading her heart in tender and silent mystery of love—the sweet, soft freshness that has bloomed on baby's limbs.

来　源

　　流泛在孩子两眼的睡眠——有谁知道它是从什么地方来的？是的，有个谣传，说它是住在萤火虫朦胧地照耀着林荫的仙村里，在那个地方，挂着两个迷人的腼怯的蓓蕾。它便是从那个地方来吻孩子的两眼的。

　　当孩子睡时，在他唇上浮动着的微笑——有谁知道它是从什么地方生出来的？是的，有个谣传，说新月的一线年轻的清光，触着将消未消的秋云边上，于是微笑便初生在一个浴在清露里的早晨的梦中了——当孩子睡时，微笑便在他的唇上浮动着。

　　甜蜜柔嫩的新鲜生气，像花一般地在孩子的四肢上开放着——有谁知道它在什么地方藏得这样久？是的，当妈妈还是一个少女的时候，它已在爱的温柔与沉静的神秘中，潜伏在她的心里了——甜蜜柔嫩的新鲜生气，像花一般地在孩子的四肢上开放着。

Baby's Way

If baby only wanted to, he could fly up to heaven this moment.

It is not for nothing that he does not leave us.

He loves to rest his head on mother's bosom, and cannot ever bear to lose sight of her.

Baby knows all manner of wise words, though few on earth can understand their meaning.

It is not for nothing that he never wants to speak.

The one thing he wants is to learn mother's words from mother's lips. That is why he looks so innocent.

Baby had a heap of gold and pearls, yet he came like a beggar on to this earth.

It is not for nothing he came in such a disguise.

孩童之道

只要孩子愿意，他此刻便可飞上天去。

他所以不离开我们，并不是没有缘故。

他爱把他的头倚在妈妈的胸间，他即使是一刻不见她，也是不行的。

孩子知道各式各样的聪明话，虽然世间的人很少懂得这些话的意义。

他所以永不想说，并不是没有缘故。

他所要做的一件事，就是要学习从妈妈的嘴唇里说出来的话。那就是他所以看来这样天真的缘故。

孩子有成堆的黄金与珠子，但他到这个世界上来，却像一个乞丐。

他所以这样假装了来，并不是没有缘故。

This dear little naked mendicant pretends to be utterly helpless, so that he may beg for mother's wealth of love.

Baby was so free from every tie in the land of the tiny crescent moon.

It was not for nothing he gave up his freedom.

He knows that there is room for endless joy in mother's little corner of a heart, and it is sweeter far than liberty to be caught and pressed in her dear arms.

Baby never knew how to cry. He dwelt in the land of perfect bliss.

It is not for nothing he has chosen to shed tears.

Though with the smile of his dear face he draws mother's yearning heart to him, yet his little cries over tiny troubles weave the double bond of pity and love.

这个可爱的小小的裸着身体的乞丐，所以假装着完全无助的样子，便是想要乞求妈妈的爱的财富。

孩子在纤小的新月的世界里，是一切束缚都没有的。

他所以放弃了他的自由，并不是没有缘故。

他知道有无穷的快乐藏在妈妈的心的小小一隅里，被妈妈亲爱的手臂所拥抱，其甜美远胜过自由。

孩子永不知道如何哭泣。他所住的是完全的乐土。

他所以要流泪，并不是没有缘故。

虽然他用了可爱的脸儿上的微笑，引逗得他妈妈的热切的心向着他，然而他的因为细故而发的小小的哭声，却编成了怜与爱的双重约束的带子。

The Unheeded Pageant

Ah, who was it coloured that little frock, my child, and covered your sweet limbs with that little red tunic?

You have come out in the morning to play in the courtyard, tottering and tumbling as you run.

But who was it coloured that little frock, my child?

What is it makes you laugh, my little life-bud?

Mother smiles at you standing on the threshold.

She claps her hands and her bracelets jingle, and you dance with your bamboo stick in your hand like a tiny little shepherd.

But what is it makes you laugh, my little life-bud?

O beggar, what do you beg for, clinging to

不被注意的花饰

啊，谁给那件小外衫染上颜色的，我的孩子，谁使你的温软的肢体穿上那件红的小外衫的？

你在早晨就跑出来到天井里玩儿，你，跑着就像摇摇欲跌似的。

但是谁给那件小外衫染上颜色的，我的孩子？

什么事叫你大笑起来的，我的小小的命芽儿？

妈妈站在门边，微笑地望着你。

她拍着她的双手，她的手镯叮当地响着；你手里拿着你的竹竿儿在跳舞，活像一个小小的牧童。

但是什么事叫你大笑起来的，我的小小的命芽儿？

喔，乞丐，你双手攀搂住妈妈的头颈，要乞讨些

your mother's neck with both your hands?

O greedy heart, shall I pluck the world like a fruit from the sky to place it on your little rosy palm?

O beggar, what are you begging for?

The wind carries away in glee the tinkling of your anklet bells.

The sun smiles and watches your toilet.

The sky watches over you when you sleep in your mother's arms, and the morning comes tiptoe to your bed and kisses your eyes.

The wind carries away in glee the tinkling of your anklet bells.

The fairy mistress of dreams is coming towards you, flying through the twilight sky.

什么？

喔，贪得无厌的心，要我把整个世界从天上摘下来，像摘一个果子似的，把它放在你的一双小小的玫瑰色的手掌上么？

喔，乞丐，你要乞讨些什么？

风高兴地带走了你踝铃的叮当。

太阳微笑着，望着你的打扮。

当你睡在你妈妈的臂弯里时，天空在上面望着你，而早晨蹑手蹑脚地走到你的床跟前，吻着你的双眼。

风高兴地带走了你踝铃的叮当。

仙乡里的梦婆飞过朦胧的天空，向你飞来。

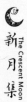

The world-mother keeps her seat by you in your mother's heart.

He who plays his music to the stars is standing at your window with his flute.

And the fairy mistress of dreams is coming towards you, flying through the twilight sky.

在你妈妈的心头上，那世界母亲，正和你坐在一块儿。

他，向星星奏乐的人，正拿着他的横笛，站在你的窗边。

仙乡里的梦婆飞过朦胧的天空，向你飞来。

Sleep-Stealer

Who stole sleep from baby's eyes? I must know.

Clasping her pitcher to her waist mother went to fetch water from the village nearby.

It was noon. The children's playtime was over; the ducks in the pond were silent.

The shepherd boy lay asleep under the shadow of the banyan tree.

The crane stood grave and still in the swamp near the mango grove.

In the meanwhile the Sleep-stealer came and, snatching sleep from baby's eyes, flew away.

When mother came back she found baby travelling the room over on all fours.

偷睡眠者

谁从孩子的眼里把睡眠偷了去呢？我一定要知道。

妈妈把她的水罐挟在腰间，走到近村汲水去了。

这是正午的时候。孩子们游戏的时间已经过去了；池中的鸭子沉默无声。

牧童躺在榕树的荫下睡着了。

白鹤庄重而安静地立在檬果树边的泥泽里。

就在这个时候，偷睡眠者跑来，从孩子的两眼里捉住睡眠，便飞去了。

当妈妈回来时，她看见孩子四肢着地地在屋里爬着。

Who stole sleep from our baby's eyes? I must know. I must find her and chain her up.

I must look into that dark cave, where, through boulders and scowling stones, trickles a tiny stream.

I must search in the drowsy shade of the bakula^① grove, where pigeons coo in their corner, and fairies' anklets tinkle in the stillness of starry nights.

In the evening I will peep into the whispering silence of the bamboo forest, where fireflies squander their light, and will ask every creature I meet, "Can anybody tell me where the Sleep-stealer lives?"

Who stole sleep from baby's eyes? I must know.

Shouldn't I give her a good lesson if I could only catch her!

I would raid her nest and see where she hoards

---

① bakula: 醉花。印度传说美女口中吐出香液，此花始开。

谁从孩子的眼里把睡眠偷了去呢？我一定要知道。我一定要找到她，把她锁起来。

我一定要向那个黑洞里张望。在这个洞里，有一道小泉从圆的和有皱纹的石上滴下来。

我一定要到醉花林中的沉寂的树影里搜寻。在这林中，鸽子在它们住的地方咕咕地叫着，仙女的脚环在繁星满天的静夜里叮当地响着。

我要在黄昏时，向静静的萧萧的竹林里窥望。在这林中，萤火虫闪闪地耗费它们的光明，只要遇见一个人，我便要问他："谁能告诉我偷睡眠者住在什么地方？"

谁从孩子的眼里把睡眠偷了去呢？我一定要知道。

只要我能捉住她，怕不会给她一顿好教训！

我要闯入她的巢穴，看她把所有偷来的睡眠藏在

all her stolen sleep.

I would plunder it all, and carry it home.

I would bind her two wings securely, set her on the bank of the river, and then let her play at fishing with a reed among the rushes and water-lilies.

When the marketing is over in the evening, and the village children sit in their mothers' laps, then the night birds will mockingly din her ears with:

"Whose sleep will you steal now?"

什么地方。

我要把它都夺来，带回家去。

我要把她的双翼缚得紧紧的，把她放在河边，然后叫她拿一根芦苇，在灯心草和睡莲间钓鱼为戏。

黄昏，街上已经收了市，村里的孩子们都坐在妈妈的膝上时，夜鸟便会讥笑地在她耳边说：

"你现在还想偷谁的睡眠呢？"

The Beginning

"Where have I come from; where did you pick me up?" the baby asked its mother.

She answered half crying, half laughing, and clasping the baby to her breast— "You were hidden in my heart as its desire, my darling.

You were in the dolls of my childhood's games; and when with clay I made the image of my god every morning, I made and unmade you then.

You were enshrined with our household deity, in his worship I worshipped you.

In all my hopes and my loves, in my life, in the life of my mother you have lived.

In the lap of the deathless Spirit who rules our home you have been nursed for ages.

开　始

"我是从哪儿来的？你，在哪儿把我捡起来的？"
孩子问他的妈妈说。

她把孩子紧紧地搂在胸前，半哭半笑地答道——
"你曾被我当作心愿藏在我的心里，我的宝贝。

"你曾存在于我孩童时代玩的泥娃娃身上；每天
早晨我用泥土塑造我的神像，那时我反复地塑了又捏
碎了的就是你。

"你曾和我们的家庭守护神一同受到祀奉，我崇
拜家神时也就崇拜了你。

"你曾活在我所有的希望和爱情里，活在我的生
命里，我母亲的生命里。

"在主宰着我们家庭的不死的精灵的膝上，你已
经被抚育了好多代了。

When in girlhood my heart was opening its petals, you hovered as a fragrance about it.

Your tender softness bloomed in my youthful limbs, like a glow in the sky before the sunrise.

Heaven's first darling, twin-born with the morning light, you have floated down the stream of the world's life, and at last you have stranded on my heart.

As I gaze on your face, mystery overwhelms me; you who belong to all have become mine.

For fear of losing you I hold you tight to my breast. What magic has snared the world's treasure in these slender arms of mine?"

"当我做女孩子的时候，我的心的花瓣儿张开，你就像一股花香似的散发出来。

"你的软软的温柔，在我青春的肢体上开花了，像太阳出来之前的天空里的一片曙光。

"上天的第一宠儿，晨曦的孪生兄弟，你从世界的生命的溪流浮泛而下，终于停泊在我的心头。

"当我凝视你的脸蛋儿的时候，神秘之感淹没了我；你这属于一切人的，竟成了我的。

"为了怕失掉你，我把你紧紧地搂在胸前。是什么魔术把这世界的宝贝引到我这双纤小的手臂里来呢？"

Baby's World

I wish I could take a quiet corner in the heart
of my baby's very own world.

I know it has stars that talk to him, and a sky
that stoops down to his face to amuse him with its
silly clouds and rainbows.

Those who make believe to be dumb, and look
as if they never could move, come creeping to his
window with their stories and with trays crowded
with bright toys.

I wish I could travel by the road that crosses
baby's mind, and out beyond all bounds;

Where messengers run errands for no cause
between the kingdoms of kings of no history;

Where Reason makes kites of her laws and
flies them, and Truth sets Fact free from its fetters.

孩子的世界

我愿我能在我孩子自己的世界的中心，占一角清净地。

我知道有星星同他说话，天空也在他面前垂下，用它呆呆的云朵和彩虹来娱悦他。

那些大家以为他是哑的人，那些看去像是永不会走动的人，都带了他们的故事，捧了满装着五颜六色的玩具的盘子，匍匐地来到他的窗前。

我愿我能在横过孩子心中的道路上游行，解脱了一切的束缚；

在那儿，使者奉了无所谓的使命奔走于无史的诸王的王国间；

在那儿，理智以它的法律造为纸鸢而飞放，真理也使事实从桎梏中自由了。

When and Why

When I bring you coloured toys, my child, I understand why there is such a play of colours on clouds, on water, and why flowers are painted in tints—when I give coloured toys to you, my child.

When I sing to make you dance, I truly know why there is music in leaves, and why waves send their chorus of voices to the heart of the listening earth—when I sing to make you dance.

When I bring sweet things to your greedy hands, I know why there is honey in the cup of the flower, and why fruits are secretly filled with sweet juice— when I bring sweet things to your greedy hands.

When I kiss your face to make you smile, my darling, I surely understand what pleasure streams from the sky in morning light, and what delight the summer breeze brings to my body—when I kiss you to make you smile.

时候与原因

当我给你五颜六色的玩具的时候，我的孩子，我明白了为什么云上水上是这样的色彩缤纷，为什么花朵上染上绚烂的颜色的原因了—— 当我给你五颜六色的玩具的时候，我的孩子。

当我唱着使你跳舞的时候，我真的知道了为什么树叶儿响着音乐，为什么波浪把它们的合唱的声音送进静听着的大地的心头的原因了—— 当我唱着使你跳舞的时候。

当我把糖果送到你贪得无厌的双手上的时候，我知道了为什么在花萼里会有蜜，为什么水果里会秘密地充溢了甜汁的原因了—— 当我把糖果送到你贪得无厌的双手上的时候。

当我吻着你的脸蛋儿叫你微笑的时候，我的宝贝，我的确明白了在晨光里从天上流下来的是什么样的快乐，而夏天的微飕吹拂在我身体上的又是什么样的爽快——当我吻着你的脸蛋儿叫你微笑的时候。

Defamation

Why are those tears in your eyes, my child?

How horrid of them to be always scolding you for nothing?

You have stained your fingers and face with ink while writing—is that why they call you dirty?

O, fie! Would they dare to call the full moon dirty because it has smudged its face with ink?

For every little trifle they blame you, my child. They are ready to find fault for nothing.

You tore your clothes while playing—is that why they call you untidy?

O, fie! What would they call an autumn morning that smiles through its ragged clouds?

责　备

为什么你眼里有了眼泪，我的孩子？

他们真是可怕，常常无谓地责备你！

你写字时墨水玷污了你的手和脸——这就是他们所以骂你龌龊的缘故么？

呵，呸！他们也敢因为圆圆的月儿用墨水涂了脸，便骂它龌龊么？

他们总要为了每一件小事去责备你，我的孩子。他们总是无谓地寻人错处。

你游戏时扯破了你的衣服——这就是他们所以说你不整洁的缘故么？

呵，呸！秋之晨从它的破碎的云衣中露出微笑，那么，他们要叫它什么呢？

Take no heed of what they say to you, my child.

Take no heed of what they say to you, my child.

They make a long list of your misdeeds. Everybody knows how you love sweet things—is that why they call you greedy?

O, fie! What then would they call us who love you?

　　他们对你说什么话，尽管可以不去理睬它，我的孩子。

　　他们把你做错的事长长地记了一笔账。

　　谁都知道你是十分喜欢糖果的—— 这就是他们所以称你做贪婪的缘故么？

　　呵，呸！我们是喜欢你的，那么，他们要叫我们什么呢？

The Judge

Say of him what you please, but I know my child's failings.

I do not love him because he is good, but because he is my little child.

How should you know how dear he can be when you try to weigh his merits against his faults?

When I must punish him he becomes all the more a part of my being.

When I cause his tears to come my heart weeps with him.

I alone have a right to blame and punish, for he only may chastise who loves.

审判官

你想说他什么尽管说吧，但是我知道我孩子的短处。

我爱他并不因为他好，只是因为他是我的小小的孩子。

你如果把他的好处与坏处两两相权，你怎会知道他是如何地可爱呢？

当我必须责罚他的时候，他更成为我的生命的一部分了。

当我使他眼泪流出时，我的心也和他同哭了。

只有我才有权去骂他，去责罚他，因为只有热爱人的才可以惩戒人。

Playthings

Child, how happy you are sitting in the dust, playing with a broken twig all the morning.

I smile at your play with that little bit of a broken twig.

I am busy with my accounts, adding up figures by the hour.

Perhaps you glance at me and think, "What a stupid game to spoil your morning with!"

Child, I have forgotten the art of being absorbed in sticks and mud-pies.

I seek out costly playthings, and gather lumps of gold and silver.

With whatever you find you create your glad games; I spend both my time and my strength over things I never can obtain.

In my frail canoe I struggle to cross the sea of desire, and forget that I too am playing a game.

玩 具

孩子，你真是快活呀！一早晨坐在泥土里，耍着折下来的小树枝儿。

我微笑地看你在那里耍弄那根折下来的小树枝儿。

我正忙着算账，一小时一小时在那里加叠数字。

也许你在看我，心想："这种好没趣的游戏，竟把你一早晨的好时间浪费掉了！"

孩子，我忘了聚精会神玩耍树枝与泥饼的方法了。

我寻求贵重的玩具，收集金块与银块。

你呢，无论找到什么便去做你的快乐的游戏；我呢，却把我的时间与力气都浪费在那些我永不能得到的东西上。

我在我的脆薄的独木船里挣扎着，要航过欲望之海，竟忘了我也是在那里做游戏了。

The Astronomer

I only said, "When in the evening the round full moon gets entangled among the branches of that Kadam[①] tree, couldn't somebody catch it?"

But dada [elder brother] laughed at me and said, "Baby, you are the silliest child I have ever known. The moon is ever so far from us; how could anybody catch it?"

I said, "Dada how foolish you are! When mother looks out of her window and smiles down at us playing, would you call her far away?"

Still dada said, "You are a stupid child! But, baby, where could you find a net big enough to catch the moon with?"

I said, "Surely you could catch it with your hands."

---

① Kadam：迦昙波。Kadam 亦作 Kadamba，意为"白花"，即昙花。

天文家

我不过说："当傍晚圆圆的满月挂在迦昙波的枝头时，有人能去捉住它么？"

哥哥却对我笑道："孩子呀，你真是我所见到的顶顶傻的孩子。月亮离我们这样远，谁能去捉住它呢？"

我说："哥哥，你真傻！当妈妈向窗外探望，微笑着往下看我们游戏时，你也能说她远么？"

哥哥还是说："你这个傻孩子！但是，孩子，你到哪里去找一个大得能逮住月亮的网呢？"

我说："你自然可以用双手去捉住它呀。"

But dada laughed and said, "You are the silliest child I have known. If it came nearer, you would see how big the moon is."

I said, "Dada, what nonsense they teach at your school! When mother bends her face down to kiss us does her face look very big?"

But still dada says, "You are a stupid child."

　　但哥哥还是笑着说："你真是我所见到的顶顶傻的孩子！如果月亮走近了，你便知道它是多么大了。"

　　我说："哥哥，你们学校里所教的，真是没有用呀！当妈妈低下脸儿跟我们亲嘴时，她的脸看来也是很大的么？"

　　但哥哥还是说："你真是一个傻孩子。"

Clouds and Waves

Mother, the folk who live up in the clouds call out to me—

"We play from the time we wake till the day ends.

We play with the golden dawn; we play with the silver moon."

I ask, "But, how am I to get up to you?" They answer, "Come to the edge of the earth, lift up your hands to the sky, and you will be taken up into the clouds."

"My mother is waiting for me at home," I say. "How can I leave her and come?"

Then they smile and float away.

But I know a nicer game than that, mother.

I shall be the cloud and you the moon.

I shall cover you with both my hands, and our

云与波

妈妈，住在云端的人对我唤道——

"我们从醒的时候游戏到白日终止。

我们与黄金色的曙光游戏，我们与银白色的月亮游戏。"

我问道："但是，我怎么能够上你那里去呢？"
他们答道："你到地球的边上来，举手向天，就可以被接到云端里来了。"

"我妈妈在家里等我呢，"我说，"我怎么能离开她而来呢？"

于是他们微笑着浮游而去。

但是我知道一件比这更好的游戏，妈妈。

我做云，你做月亮。

我用两只手遮盖你，我们的屋顶就是青碧的天空。

house-top will be the blue sky.

The folk who live in the waves call out to me—

"We sing from morning till night; on and on we travel and know not where we pass."

I ask, "But, how am I to join you?"

They tell me, "Come to the edge of the shore and stand with your eyes tight shut, and you will be carried out upon the waves."

I say, "My mother always wants me at home in the evening—how can I leave her and go?"

Then they smile, dance and pass by.

But I know a better game than that.

I will be the waves and you will be a strange shore.

I shall roll on and on and on, and break upon your lap with laughter.

And no one in the world will know where we both are.

住在波浪上的人对我唤道——

"我们从早晨唱歌到晚上；我们前进又前进地旅行，也不知我们所经过的是什么地方。"

我问道："但是，我怎么才能加入你们队伍里呢？"

他们告诉我说："来到岸旁，站在那里，紧闭你的两眼，你就被带到波浪上来了。"

我说："傍晚的时候，我妈妈常要我在家里——我怎么能离开她而去呢？"

于是他们微笑着，跳着舞奔流过去。

但是我知道一件比这更好的游戏。

我是波浪，你是陌生的岸。

我奔流而进，进，进，笑哈哈地撞碎在你的膝上。

世界上就没有一个人会知道我们俩在什么地方。

The Champa Flower

Supposing I became a champa [①] flower, just for fun, and grew on a branch high up that tree, and shook in the wind with laughter and danced upon the newly budded leaves, would you know me, mother?

You would call, "Baby, where are you?" and I should laugh to myself and keep quite quiet.

I should slyly open my petals and watch you at your work.

When after your bath, with wet hair spread on your shoulders, you walked through the shadow of the champa tree to the little court where you say your prayers, you would notice the scent of the flower, but not know that it came from me.

When after the midday meal you sat at the window

---

① champa：金色花。印度圣树，木兰花属植物，开金黄色碎花。

金色花

假如我变了一朵金色花，只是为了好玩，长在那棵树的高枝上，笑哈哈地在风中摇摆，又在新生的树叶上跳舞，妈妈，你会认识我么？

你要是叫道："孩子，你在哪里呀？"我暗暗地在那里匿笑，却一声儿不响。

我要悄悄地开放花瓣儿，看着你工作。

当你沐浴后，湿发披在两肩，穿过金色花的林荫，走到你做祷告的小庭院时，你会嗅到这花的香气，却不知道这香气是从我身上来的。

当你吃过中饭，坐在窗前读《罗摩衍那》，那棵

reading *Ramayana*① , and the tree's shadow fell over your hair and your lap, I should fling my wee little shadow on to the page of your book, just where you were reading.

But would you guess that it was the tiny shadow of your little child?

When in the evening you went to the cow-shed with the lighted lamp in your hand, I should suddenly drop on to the earth again and be your own baby once more, and beg you to tell me a story.

"Where have you been, you naughty child?"

"I won't tell you, mother." That's what you and I would say then.

---

① *Ramayana*: 《罗摩衍那》, 印度叙事诗, 相传系蚁垤 (跋弥) (Valmiki) 所作。全文共分为七章, 主要讲述了阿逾陀国王子罗摩 (Rama) 和他妻子悉多 (Sita) 的故事。

树的阴影落在你的头发与膝上时，我便要投我的小小
的影子在你的书页上，正投在你所读的地方。

但是你会猜得出这就是你孩子的小小影子么？

当你黄昏时拿了灯到牛棚里去，我便要突然地再
落到地上来，又成了你的孩子，求你讲个故事给我听。

"你到哪里去了，你这坏孩子？"

"我不告诉你，妈妈。"这就是你同我那时所要
说的话了。

The Crescent Moon
新
月
集

Fairyland

If people came to know where my king's palace is, it would vanish into the air.

The walls are of white silver and the roof of shining gold.

The queen lives in a palace with seven courtyards, and she wears a jewel that cost all the wealth of seven kingdoms.

But let me tell you, mother, in a whisper, where my king's palace is.

It is at the corner of our terrace where the pot of the tulsi plant stands.

The princess lies sleeping on the far-away shore of the seven impassable seas.

仙人世界

如果人们知道了我的国王的宫殿在哪里，它就会消失在空气中的。

墙壁是白色的银，屋顶是耀眼的黄金。

皇后住在有七个庭院的宫苑里；她戴的一串珠宝，值得整整七个王国的全部财富。

不过，让我悄悄地告诉你，妈妈，我的国王的宫殿究竟在哪里。

它就在我们阳台的角上，在那栽着杜尔茜花的花盆放着的地方。

公主躺在远远的、隔着七个不可逾越的重洋的那一岸沉睡着。

There is none in the world who can find her but myself.

She has bracelets on her arms and pearl drops in her ears; her hair sweeps down upon the floor.

She will wake when I touch her with my magic wand, and jewels will fall from her lips when she smiles.

But let me whisper in your ear, mother; she is there in the corner of our terrace where the pot of the tulsi plant stands.

When it is time for you to go to the river for your bath, step up to that terrace on the roof.

I sit in the corner where the shadows of the walls meet together.

Only puss is allowed to come with me, for she

除了我自己，世界上便没有人能够找到她。

她臂上有镯子，她耳上挂着珍珠，她的头发拖到
地板上。

当我用我的魔杖点触她的时候，她就会醒过来；
而当她微笑时，珠玉将会从她唇边落下来。

不过，让我在你的耳朵边悄悄地告诉你，妈妈，
她就住在我们阳台的角上，在那栽着杜尔茜花的花盆
放着的地方。

当你要到河里洗澡的时候，你走上屋顶的那座阳
台来吧。

我就坐在墙的阴影所聚会的一个角落里。

我只让小猫儿跟我在一起，因为它知道那故事里

知 The Crescent Moon 月 集

knows where the barber in the story lives.

But let me whisper, mother, in your ear where the barber in the story lives.

It is at the corner of the terrace where the pot of the tulsi plant stands.

的理发匠住的地方。

不过，让我在你的耳朵边悄悄地告诉你，那故事里的理发匠到底住在哪里。

他住的地方，就在阳台的角上，在那栽着杜尔茜花的花盆放着的地方。

The Land of the Exile

Mother, the light has grown grey in the sky; I do not know what the time is.

There is no fun in my play, so I have come to you. It is Saturday, our holiday.

Leave off your work, mother; sit here by the window and tell me where the desert of Tepantar in the fairy tale is.

The shadow of the rains has covered the day from end to end.

The fierce lightning is scratching the sky with its nails.

When the clouds rumble and it thunders, I love to be afraid in my heart and cling to you.

流放的地方

妈妈，天空上的光成了灰色了；我不知道是什么时候了。

我玩得怪没劲儿的，所以到你这里来了。这是星期六，是我们的休息日。

放下你的活计，妈妈，坐在靠窗的一边，告诉我童话里的特潘塔沙漠在什么地方。

雨的影子遮掩了整个白天。

凶猛的电光用它的爪子抓着天空。

当乌云在轰轰地响着，天打着雷的时候，我总爱心里带着恐惧爬伏到你的身上。

When the heavy rain patters for hours on the bamboo leaves, and our windows shake and rattle at the gusts of wind, I like to sit alone in the room, mother, with you, and hear you talk about the desert of Tepantar in the fairy tale.

Where is it, mother, on the shore of what sea, at the foot of what hills, in the kingdom of what king?

There are no hedges there to mark the fields, no footpath across it by which the villagers reach their village in the evening, or the woman who gathers dry sticks in the forest can bring her load to the market. With patches of yellow grass in the sand and only one tree where the pair of wise old birds have their nest, lies the desert of Tepantar.

I can imagine how, on just such a cloudy day, the young son of the king is riding alone on a grey horse through the desert, in search of the princess who lies imprisoned in the giant's palace across that unknown water.

当大雨倾泻在竹叶子上好几个钟头，而我们的窗户为狂风震得格格发响的时候，我就爱独自和你坐在屋里，妈妈，听你讲童话里的特潘塔沙漠的故事。

它在哪里，妈妈，在哪一个海洋的岸上？在哪些个山峰的脚下？在哪一个国王的国土里？

田地上没有此疆彼壤的界石，也没有村人在黄昏时走回家的或妇人在树林里捡拾枯枝而捆载到市场上去的道路。沙地上只有一小块一小块的黄色草地，只有一株树，就是那一对聪明的老鸟儿在那里做窝的，那个地方就是特潘塔沙漠。

我能够想象得到，就在这样一个乌云密布的日子，国王的年轻的儿子，怎样独自骑着一匹灰色马，走过这个沙漠，去寻找那被囚禁在不可知的重洋之外的巨人宫里的公主。

When the haze of the rain comes down in the distant sky, and lightning starts up like a sudden fit of pain, does he remember his unhappy mother, abandoned by the king, sweeping the cow-stall and wiping her eyes, while he rides through the desert of Tepantar in the fairy tale?

See, mother, it is almost dark before the day is over, and there are no travellers yonder on the village road.

The shepherd boy has gone home early from the pasture, and men have left their fields to sit on mats under the eaves of their huts, watching the scowling clouds.

Mother, I have left all my books on the shelf— do not ask me to do my lessons now.

When I grow up and am big like my father, I shall learn all that must be learned.

But just for today, tell me, mother, where the desert of Tepantar in the fairy tale is?

当雨雾在遥远的天空下降，电光像一阵突然发作的痛楚的痉挛似的闪射的时候，他可记得他的不幸的母亲，为国王所弃，正在打扫牛棚，眼里流着眼泪，当他骑马走过童话里的特潘塔沙漠的时候？

看，妈妈，一天还没有完，天色就差不多黑了，那边村庄的路上没有什么旅客了。

牧童早就从牧场上回家了，人们都已从田地里回来，坐在他们草屋檐下的草席上，眼望着阴沉的云块。

妈妈，我把我所有的书本都放在书架上了——不要叫我现在做功课。

当我长大了，大得像爸爸一样的时候，我将会学到必须学到的东西的。

但是，今天你可得告诉我，妈妈，童话里的特潘塔沙漠在什么地方？

The Rainy Day

Sullen clouds are gathering fast over the black fringe of the forest.

O child, do not go out!

The palm trees in a row by the lake are smiting their heads against the dismal sky; the crows with their draggled wings are silent on the tamarind branches, and the eastern bank of the river is haunted by a deepening gloom.

Our cow is lowing loud, tied at the fence.

O child, wait here till I bring her into the stall.

Men have crowded into the flooded field to catch the fishes as they escape from the overflowing ponds; the rain water is running in rills through the narrow lanes like a laughing boy who has run away from his mother to tease her.

雨 天

乌云很快地集拢在森林的黝黑的边缘上。

孩子，不要出去呀！

湖边的一行棕树，向暝暗的天空撞着头；羽毛零乱的乌鸦，静悄悄地栖在罗望子树的枝上。河的东岸正被乌沉沉的暝色所侵袭。

我们的牛系在篱上，高声鸣叫。

孩子，在这里等着，等我先把牛牵进牛棚里去。

许多人都挤在池水泛溢的田间，捉那从泛溢的池中逃出来的鱼儿。雨水成了小河，流过狭街，好像一个嬉笑的孩子从他妈妈那里跑开，故意要恼她一样。

Listen, someone is shouting for the boatman at the ford.

O child, the daylight is dim, and the crossing at the ferry is closed.

The sky seems to ride fast upon the madly-rushing rain; the water in the river is loud and impatient; women have hastened home early from the Ganges with their filled pitchers.

The evening lamps must be made ready.

O child, do not go out!

The road to the market is desolate; the lane to the river is slippery. The wind is roaring and struggling among the bamboo branches like a wild beast tangled in a net.

听呀，有人在浅滩上喊船夫呢。

孩子，天色暝暗了，渡头的摆渡船已经停了。

天空好像是在滂沱的雨上快跑着；河里的水喧叫而且暴躁；妇人们早已拿着汲满了水的水罐，从恒河畔匆匆地回家了。

夜里用的灯，一定要预备好。

孩子，不要出去呀！

到市场去的大道已没有人走，到河边去的小路又很滑。风在竹林里咆哮着，挣扎着，好像一只落在网中的野兽。

Paper Boats

Day by day I float my paper boats one by one down the running stream.

In big black letters I write my name on them and the name of the village where I live.

I hope that someone in some strange land will find them and know who I am.

I load my little boats with shiuli flowers from our garden, and hope that these blooms of the dawn will be carried safely to land in the night.

I launch my paper boats and look up into the sky and see the little clouds setting their white bulging sails.

I know not what playmate of mine in the sky sends them down the air to race with my boats!

纸 船

我每天把纸船一个个放在急流的溪中。

我用大黑字把我的名字和我住的村名写在纸船上。

我希望住在异地的人会得到这纸船，知道我是谁。

我把园中长的秀利花载在我的小船上，希望这些黎明开的花能在夜里被平平安安地带到岸上。

我把我的纸船投到水里，仰望天空，看见小朵的云正张着满鼓着风的白帆。

我不知道天上有我的什么游伴把这些船放下来同我的船比赛！

When night comes I bury my face in my arms and dream that my paper boats float on and on under the midnight stars.

The fairies of sleep are sailing in them, and the lading is their baskets full of dreams.

夜来了，我的脸埋在手臂里，梦见我的纸船在子夜的星光下缓缓地浮泛向前。

睡仙坐在船里，带着满载着梦的篮子。

The Sailor

The boat of the boatman Madhu is moored at the wharf of Rajgunj.

It is uselessly laden with jute, and has been lying there idle for ever so long.

If he would only lend me his boat, I should man her with a hundred oars, and hoist sails, five or six or seven.

I should never steer her to stupid markets. I should sail the seven seas and the thirteen rivers of fairyland.

But, mother, you won't weep for me in a corner.

I am not going into the forest like Ramachandra[1] to come back only after fourteen years.

---

① Ramachandra: 罗摩犍陀罗，即罗摩。他是印度叙事诗《罗摩衍那》中的主角。为了尊重父亲的诺言和维持弟兄间的友爱，他放弃了继承王位的权利，和妻子悉多在森林中被放逐了十四年。

水 手

船夫曼特胡的船只停泊在拉琪根琪码头。

这只船无用地装载着黄麻，无所事事地停泊在那里已经好久了。

只要他肯把他的船借给我，我就给它安装一百只桨，扬起五个或六个或七个布帆来。

我决不把它驾驶到愚蠢的市场上去。我将航行遍仙人世界里的七个大海和十三条河道。

但是，妈妈，你不会躲在角落里为我哭泣。

我不会像罗摩犍陀罗似的，到森林中去，一去十四年才回来。

I shall become the prince of the story, and fill my boat with whatever I like.

I shall take my friend Ashu with me. We shall sail merrily across the seven seas and the thirteen rivers of fairyland.

We shall set sail in the early morning light.

When at noontide you are bathing at the pond, we shall be in the land of a strange king.

We shall pass the ford of Tirpurni, and leave behind us the desert of Tepantar.

When we come back it will be getting dark, and I shall tell you of all that we have seen.

I shall cross the seven seas and the thirteen rivers of fairyland.

　　我将成为故事中的王子，把我的船装满了我所喜欢的东西。

　　我将带我的朋友阿细和我做伴。我们要快快乐乐地航行于仙人世界里的七个大海和十三条河道。

　　我将在绝早的晨光里张帆航行。

　　中午，你正在池塘里洗澡的时候，我们将在一个陌生的国王的国土上了。

　　我们将经过特浦尼浅滩，把特潘塔沙漠抛落在我们的后边。

　　当我们回来的时候，天色快黑了，我将告诉你我们所见到的一切。

　　我将越过仙人世界里的七个大海和十三条河道。

The Further Bank

I long to go over there to the further bank of the river,

Where those boats are tied to the bamboo poles in a line;

Where men cross over in their boats in the morning with ploughs on their shoulders to till their far-away fields;

Where the cowherds make their lowing cattle swim across to the riverside pasture;

Whence they all come back home in the evening, leaving the jackals to howl in the island overgrown with weeds.

Mother, if you don't mind, I should like to become the boatman of the ferry when I am grown up.

对 岸

我渴想到河的对岸去。

在那边，好些船只一行儿系在竹竿上；

人们在早晨乘船渡过那边去，肩上扛着犁头，去耕耘他们的远处的田；

在那边，牧人使他们哞叫着的牛游泳到河旁的牧场去；

黄昏的时候，他们都回家了，只留下豺狼在这满长着野草的岛上哀叫。

妈妈，如果你不在意，我长大的时候，要做这渡船的船夫。

They say there are strange pools hidden behind that high bank,

Where flocks of wild ducks come when the rains are over, and thick reeds grow round the margins where waterbirds lay their eggs;

Where snipes with their dancing tails stamp their tiny footprints upon the clean soft mud;

Where in the evening the tall grasses crested with white flowers invite the moonbeam to float upon their waves.

Mother, if you don't mind, I should like to become the boatman of the ferryboat when I am grown up.

I shall cross and cross back from bank to bank, and all the boys and girls of the village will wonder at me while they are bathing.

据说有好些古怪的池塘藏在这个高岸之后。

雨过去了，一群一群的野鹜飞到那里去。茂盛的芦苇在岸边四围生长，水鸟在那里生蛋；

竹鸡带着跳舞的尾巴，将它们细小的足印印在洁净的软泥上；

黄昏的时候，长草顶着白花，邀月光在长草的波浪上浮游。

妈妈，如果你不在意，我长大的时候，要做这渡船的船夫。

我要自此岸至彼岸，渡过来，渡过去，所有村中正在那儿沐浴的男孩女孩，都要诧异地望着我。

When the sun climbs the mid sky and morning wears on to noon, I shall come running to you, saying, "Mother, I am hungry!"

When the day is done and the shadows cower under the trees, I shall come back in the dusk.

I shall never go away from you into the town to work like father.

Mother, if you don't mind, I should like to become the boatman of the ferryboat when I am grown up.

太阳升到中天，早晨变为正午了，我将跑到你那里去，说道："妈妈，我饿了！"

一天完了，影子俯伏在树底下，我便要在黄昏中回家来。

我将永不像爸爸那样，离开你到城里去做事。

妈妈，如果你不在意，我长大的时候，要做这渡船的船夫。

The Flower-School

When storm clouds rumble in the sky and June showers come down, The moist east wind comes marching over the heath to blow its bagpipes among the bamboos.

Then crowds of flowers come out of a sudden, from nobody knows where, and dance upon the grass in wild glee.

Mother, I really think the flowers go to school underground.

They do their lessons with doors shut, and if they want to come out to play before it is time, their master makes them stand in a corner.

When the rains come they have their holidays.

花的学校

当雷云在天上轰响，六月的阵雨落下的时候，润湿的东风走过荒野，在竹林中吹着口笛。

于是一群一群的花从无人知道的地方突然跑出来，在绿草上狂欢地跳着舞。

妈妈，我真的觉得那群花朵是在地下的学校里上学。

它们关了门做功课，如果它们想在散学以前出来游戏，它们的老师是要罚它们站壁角的。

雨一来，它们便放假了。

新
月
集
The Crescent Moon

Branches clash together in the forest, and the leaves rustle in the wild wind, the thunder-clouds clap their giant hands and the flower children rush out in dresses of pink and yellow and white.

Do you know, mother, their home is in the sky, where the stars are.

Haven't you seen how eager they are to get there? Don't you know why they are in such a hurry?

Of course, I can guess to whom they raise their arms: they have their mother as I have my own.

树枝在林中互相碰触着，绿叶在狂风里萧萧地响着，雷云拍着大手。这时花孩子们便穿了紫的、黄的、白的衣裳，冲了出来。

你可知道，妈妈，它们的家是在天上，在星星所住的地方。

你没有看见它们怎样地急着要到那儿去么？你不知道它们为什么那样急急忙忙么？

我自然能够猜得出它们是对谁扬起双臂来：它们也有它们的妈妈，就像我有我自己的妈妈一样。

The Merchant

Imagine, mother, that you are to stay at home and I am to travel into strange lands.

Imagine that my boat is ready at the landing fully laden.

Now think well, mother, before you say what I shall bring for you when I come back.

Mother, do you want heaps and heaps of gold?

There, by the banks of golden streams, fields are full of golden harvest.

And in the shade of the forest path the golden champa flowers drop on the ground.

I will gather them all for you in many hundred baskets.

商　人

妈妈，让我们想象，你待在家里，我到异邦去旅行。

再想象，我的船已经装得满满的，在码头上等候启碇了。

现在，妈妈，你想一想告诉我，回来时我要带些什么给你。

妈妈，你要一堆一堆的黄金么？

在金河的两岸，田野里全是金色的稻实。

在林荫的路上，金色花也一朵一朵地落在地上。

我要为你把它们全都收拾起来，放在好几百个篮子里。

Mother, do you want pearls big as the raindrops of autumn?

I shall cross to the pearl island shore. There in the early morning light pearls tremble on the meadow flowers, pearls drop on the grass, and pearls are scattered on the sand in spray by the wild sea-waves.

My brother shall have a pair of horses with wings to fly among the clouds.

For father I shall bring a magic pen that, without his knowing, will write of itself.

For you, mother, I must have the casket and jewel that cost seven kings their kingdoms.

妈妈，你要秋天的雨点一般大的珍珠么？

我要渡海到珍珠岛的岸上去。那个地方，在清晨的曙光里，珠子在草地的野花上颤动，珠子落在绿草上，珠子被汹狂的海浪一大把一大把地撒在沙滩上。

我的哥哥呢，我要送他一对有翼的马，会在云端飞翔的。

爸爸呢，我要带一支有魔力的笔给他，他还没有感觉到，笔就写出字来了。

你呢，妈妈，我要把值七个王国的首饰箱和珠宝送给你。

Sympathy

If I were only a little puppy, not your baby, mother dear, would you say "No" to me if I tried to eat from your dish?

Would you drive me off, saying to me, "Get away, you naughty little puppy?"

Then go, mother, go! I will never come to you when you call me, and never let you feed me any more.

If I were only a little green parrot, and not your baby, mother dear, would you keep me chained lest I should fly away?

Would you shake your finger at me and say, "What an ungrateful wretch of a bird! It is gnawing at its chain day and night?"

Then, go, mother, go! I will run away into the woods; I will never let you take me in your arms again.

同　情

　　如果我只是一只小狗，而不是你的小孩，亲爱的妈妈，当我想吃你盘里的东西时，你要向我说"不"么？

　　你要赶开我，对我说道"滚开，你这淘气的小狗"么？

　　那么，走吧，妈妈，走吧！当你叫唤我的时候，我就永不到你那里去，也永不要你再喂我吃东西了。

　　如果我只是一只绿色的小鹦鹉，而不是你的小孩，亲爱的妈妈，你要把我紧紧地锁住，怕我飞走么？

　　你要对我指指点点地说道"怎样的一只不知感恩的贱鸟呀！整日整夜地尽在咬它的链子"么？

　　那么，走吧，妈妈，走吧！我要跑到树林里去；我就永不再让你将我抱在你的臂里了。

Vocation

When the gong sounds ten in the morning and I walk to school by our lane,

Every day I meet the hawker crying, "Bangles, crystal bangles!"

There is nothing to hurry him on; there is no road he must take, no place he must go to, no time when he must come home.

I wish I were a hawker, spending my day in the road, crying, "Bangles, crystal bangles!"

When at four in the afternoon I come back from the school.

I can see through the gate of that house the gardener digging the ground.

职 业

早晨，钟敲十下的时候，我沿着我们的小巷到学校去。

每天我都遇见那个小贩，他叫道："镯子呀，亮晶晶的镯子！"

他没有什么事情急着要做，他没有哪条街一定要走，他没有什么地方一定要去，他没有什么规定的时间一定要回家。

我愿意我是一个小贩，在街上过日子，叫着："镯子呀，亮晶晶的镯子！"

下午四点钟，我从学校里回家。

从一家门口，我看见一个园丁在那里掘地。

He does what he likes with his spade; he soils his clothes with dust; nobody takes him to task if he gets baked in the sun or gets wet.

I wish I were a gardener digging away at the garden with nobody to stop me from digging.

Just as it gets dark in the evening and my mother sends me to bed.

I can see through my open window the watchman walking up and down.

The lane is dark and lonely, and the street-lamp stands like a giant with one red eye in its head.

The watchman swings his lantern and walks with his shadow at his side, and never once goes to bed in his life.

I wish I were a watchman walking the streets all night, chasing the shadows with my lantern.

他用他的锄子，要怎么掘，便怎么掘，他被尘土污了衣裳。如果他被太阳晒黑了或是身上被打湿了，都没有人骂他。

我愿意我是一个园丁，在花园里掘地，谁也不来阻止我。

天色刚黑，妈妈就送我上床。

从开着的窗口，我看见更夫走来走去。

小巷又黑又冷清，路灯立在那里，像一个头上生着一只红眼睛的巨人。

更夫摇着他的提灯，跟他身边的影子一起走着，他一生一次都没有上床去过。

我愿意我是一个更夫，整夜在街上走，提了灯去追逐影子。

Superior

Mother, your baby is silly! She is so absurdly childish!

She does not know the difference between the lights in the streets and the stars.

When we play at eating with pebbles, she thinks they are real food, and tries to put them into her mouth.

When I open a book before her and ask her to learn her a, b, c, she tears the leaves with her hands and roars for joy at nothing; this is your baby's way of doing her lesson.

When I shake my head at her in anger and scold her and call her naughty, she laughs and thinks it great fun.

长 者

妈妈，你的孩子真傻！她是那么可笑地不懂事！

她不知道路灯和星星的分别。

当我们玩着把小石子当食物的游戏时，她便以为它们真是吃的东西，竟想放进嘴里去。

当我翻开一本书，放在她面前，要她读 a，b，c 时，她却用手把书页撕了，无端快活地叫起来；你的孩子就是这样做功课的。

当我生气地对她摇头，骂她，说她顽皮时，她却哈哈大笑，以为很有趣。

Everybody knows that father is away, but if in play I call aloud "Father," she looks about her in excitement and thinks that father is near.

When I hold my class with the donkeys that our washerman brings to carry away the clothes and I warn her that I am the schoolmaster, she will scream for no reason and call me dada.

Your baby wants to catch the moon. She is so funny; she calls Ganesh[①] Ganush.

Mother, your baby is silly; she is so absurdly childish!

---

① Ganesh: 格尼许，是毁灭之神湿婆的儿子，象头人身。这个名字
也是现代印度人起名时最喜欢用的。

谁都知道爸爸不在家，但是，如果我在游戏时高叫一声"爸爸"，她便要高兴地四面张望，以为爸爸真是近在身边。

当我把洗衣人带来载衣服回去的驴子当作学生，并且警告她说，我是老师时，她却无缘无故地乱叫起我哥哥来。

你的孩子要捉月亮。她是这样的可笑；她把格尼许唤做琪奴许。

妈妈，你的孩子真傻，她是那么可笑地不懂事！

The Little Big Man

I am small because I am a little child. I shall be big when I am as old as my father is.

My teacher will come and say, "It is late; bring your slate and your books."

I shall tell him, "Do you not know I am as big as father? And I must not have lessons any more."

My master will wonder and say, "He can leave his books if he likes, for he is grown up."

I shall dress myself and walk to the fair where the crowd is thick.

My uncle will come rushing up to me and say, "You will get lost, my boy; let me carry you."

小大人

我人很小，因为我是一个小孩子。到了我像爸爸一样年纪时，便要变大了。

我的先生要是走来说道："时候晚了，把你的石板、你的书拿来。"

我便要告诉他道："你不知道我已经同爸爸一样大了么？我决不再学什么功课了。"

我的老师便将惊异地说道："他读书不读书可以随便，因为他是大人了。"

我将自己穿了衣裳，走到人群拥挤的市场里去。

我的叔叔要是跑过来说道："你要迷路了，我的孩子，让我领着你吧。"

I shall answer, "Can't you see, uncle, I am as big as father? I must go to the fair alone."

Uncle will say, "Yes, he can go wherever he likes, for he is grown up."

Mother will come from her bath when I am giving money to my nurse, for I shall know how to open the box with my key.

Mother will say, "What are you about, naughty child?"

I shall tell her, "Mother, don't you know, I am as big as father, and I must give silver to my nurse."

Mother will say to herself, "He can give money to whom he likes, for he is grown up."

In the holiday time in October father will come home and, thinking that I am still a baby, will bring for me from the town little shoes and small silken frocks.

我便要回答道："你没有看见么，叔叔？我已经同爸爸一样大了。我决定要独自一人到市场里去。"

叔叔便将说道："是的，他随便到哪里去都可以，因为他是大人了。"

当我正拿钱给我保姆时，妈妈便要从浴室中出来，因为我是知道怎样用我的钥匙去开银箱的。

妈妈要是说道："你在做什么呀，顽皮的孩子？"

我便要告诉她道："妈妈，你不知道我已经同爸爸一样大了么？我必须拿钱给保姆。"

妈妈便将自言自语道："他可以随便把钱给他所喜欢的人，因为他是大人了。"

当十月里放假的时候，爸爸将要回家，他会以为我还是一个小孩子，为我从城里带了小鞋子和小绸衫来。

I shall say, "Father, give them to my dada, for I am as big as you are."

Father will think and say, "He can buy his own clothes if he likes, for he is grown up."

　　我便要说道："爸爸，把这些东西给哥哥吧，因为我已经同你一样大了。"

　　爸爸便将想一想，说道："他可以随便去买他自己穿的衣裳，因为他是大人了。"

Twelve O'clock

Mother, I do want to leave off my lessons now.
I have been at my book all the morning.

You say it is only twelve o'clock. Suppose it
isn't any later; can't you ever think it is afternoon
when it is only twelve o'clock?

I can easily imagine now that the sun has
reached the edge of that rice-field, and the old
fisher-woman is gathering herbs for her supper by
the side of the pond.

I can just shut my eyes and think that the
shadows are growing darker under the madar tree,
and the water in the pond looks shiny black.

If twelve o'clock can come in the night, why
can't the night come when it is twelve o'clock?

十二点钟

妈妈，我真想现在不做功课了。我整个早晨都在念书呢。

你说，现在还不过是十二点钟。假定不会晚过十二点吧；难道你不能把不过是十二点钟想象成下午么？

我能够很容易地想象：现在太阳已经到了那片稻田的边缘上了，老态龙钟的渔婆正在池边采撷香草做她的晚餐。

我闭上了眼就能够想到，马塔尔树下的阴影是更深黑了，池塘里的水看来黑得发亮。

假如十二点钟能够在黑夜里来到，为什么黑夜不能在十二点钟的时候来到呢？

Authorship

You say that father writes a lot of books, but what he writes I don't understand.

He was reading to you all the evening, but could you really make out what he meant?

What nice stories, mother, you can tell us! Why can't father write like that, I wonder?

Did he never hear from his own mother stories of giants and fairies and princesses?

Has he forgotten them all?

Often when he gets late for his bath you have to go and call him a hundred times.

You wait and keep his dishes warm for him, but he goes on writing and forgets.

Father always plays at making books.

著作家

你说爸爸写了许多书，但我却不懂得他所写的东西。

他整个黄昏读书给你听，但是你真懂得他的意思么？

妈妈，你给我们讲的故事，真是好听呀！我很奇怪，爸爸为什么不能写那样的书呢？

难道他从来没有从他自己的妈妈那里听见过巨人、神仙和公主的故事么？

还是已经完全忘记了？

他常常耽误了沐浴，你不得不走去叫他一百多次。

你总要等候着，把他的菜温着等他，但他忘了，还尽管写下去。

爸爸老是以著书为游戏。

If ever I go to play in father's room, you come and call me, "What a naughty child!"

If I make the slightest noise, you say, "Don't you see that father's at his work?"

What's the fun of always writing and writing?

When I take up father's pen or pencil and write upon his book just as he does—a, b, c, d, e, f, g, h, i—why do you get cross with me, then, mother?

You never say a word when father writes.

When my father wastes such heaps of paper, mother, you don't seem to mind at all.

But if I take only one sheet to make a boat with, you say, "Child, how troublesome you are!"

What do you think of father's spoiling sheets and sheets of paper with black marks all over on both sides?

如果我一走进爸爸房里去游戏,你就要走来叫道:"真是一个顽皮的孩子!"

如果我稍微弄出一点声音,你就要说:"你没有看见你爸爸正在工作么?"

老是写了又写,有什么趣味呢?

当我拿起爸爸的钢笔或铅笔,像他一模一样地在他的书上写着a,b,c,d,e,f,g,h,i——那时,你为什么跟我生气呢,妈妈?

爸爸写时,你却从来不说一句话。

当我爸爸耗费了那么一大堆纸时,妈妈,你似乎全不在乎。

但是,如果我只取了一张纸去做一只船,你却要说,"孩子,你真讨厌!"

你对于爸爸拿黑点子涂满了纸的两面,污损了许多许多张纸,心里以为怎样呢?

The Wicked Postman

Why do you sit there on the floor so quiet and silent, tell me, mother dear?

The rain is coming in through the open window, making you all wet, and you don't mind it.

Do you hear the gong striking four? It is time for my brother to come home from school.

What has happened to you that you look so strange?

Haven't you got a letter from father today?

I saw the postman bringing letters in his bag for almost everybody in the town.

Only, father's letters he keeps to read himself. I am sure the postman is a wicked man.

But don't be unhappy about that, mother dear.

Tomorrow is market day in the next village.

恶邮差

你为什么坐在那边地板上不言不动的？告诉我呀，亲爱的妈妈。

雨从开着的窗口打进来了，把你身上全打湿了，你却不管。

你听见钟已打了四下么？正是哥哥从学校里回家的时候了。

到底发生了什么事，你的神色这样不对？

你今天没有接到爸爸的信么？

我看见邮差在他的袋里带了许多信来，几乎镇里的每个人都分送到了。

只有爸爸的信，他留起来给他自己看。我确信这个邮差是个坏人。

但是不要因此不乐呀，亲爱的妈妈。

明天是邻村市集的日子。你叫女仆去买些笔和

You ask your maid to buy some pens and paper.

I myself will write all father's letters; you will not find a single mistake.

I shall write from A right up to K.

But, mother, why do you smile?

You don't believe that I can write as nicely as father does!

But I shall rule my paper carefully, and write all the letters beautifully big.

When I finish my writing, do you think I shall be so foolish as father and drop it into the horrid postman's bag?

I shall bring it to you myself without waiting, and letter by letter help you to read my writing.

I know the postman does not like to give you the really nice letters.

ize.

纸来。

我自己会写爸爸所写的一切信，使你找不出一点错处来。

我要从 A 字一直写到 K 字。

但是，妈妈，你为什么笑呢？

你不相信我能写得像爸爸一样好？

但是我将用心画格子，把所有的字母都写得又大又美。

当我写好了时，你以为我也像爸爸那样傻，把它投入可怕的邮差的袋中么？

我立刻就自己送来给你，而且一个字母、一个字母地帮助你读。

我知道那邮差是不肯把真正的好信送给你的。

The Hero

Mother, let us imagine we are travelling, and passing through a strange and dangerous country.

You are riding in a palanquin and I am trotting by you on a red horse.

It is evening and the sun goes down. The waste of Joradighi lies wan and grey before us. The land is desolate and barren.

You are frightened and thinking—"I know not where we have come to."

I say to you, "Mother, do not be afraid."

The meadow is prickly with spiky grass, and through it runs a narrow broken path.

There are no cattle to be seen in the wide field;

英　雄

妈妈，让我们想象我们正在旅行，经过一个陌生而危险的国土。

你坐在一顶轿子里，我骑着一匹红马，在你旁边跑着。

是黄昏的时候，太阳已经下山了。约拉地希的荒地疲乏而灰暗地展开在我们面前，大地是凄凉而荒芜的。

你害怕了，想道——"我不知道我们到了什么地方了。"

我对你说道："妈妈，不要害怕。"

草地上刺蓬蓬地长着针尖似的草，一条狭而崎岖的小道通过这块草地。

在这片广大的地面上看不见一只牛；它们已经回

they have gone to their village stalls.

It grows dark and dim on the land and sky, and we cannot tell where we are going.

Suddenly you call me and ask me in a whisper, "What light is that near the bank?"

Just then there bursts out a fearful yell, and figures come running towards us.

You sit crouched in your palanquin and repeat the names of the gods in prayer.

The bearers, shaking in terror, hide themselves in the thorny bush.

I shout to you, "Don't be afraid, mother. I am here."

With long sticks in their hands and hair all wild about their heads, they come nearer and nearer.

到它们村里的牛棚去了。

天色黑了下来，大地和天空都显得朦朦胧胧的，
而我们不能说出我们正走向什么所在。

突然间，你叫我，悄悄地问我道："靠近河岸的
是什么火光呀？"

正在那个时候，一阵可怕的呐喊声爆发了，好些
人影子向我们跑过来。

你蹲坐在你的轿子里，嘴里反复地祷念着神的
名字。

轿夫们，怕得发抖，躲藏在荆棘丛中。

我向你喊道："不要害怕，妈妈，有我在这里。"

他们手里执着长棒，头发披散着，越走越近了。

I shout, "Have a care! You villains! One step more and you are dead men."

They give another terrible yell and rush forward.

You clutch my hand and say, "Dear boy, for heaven's sake, keep away from them."

I say, "Mother, just you watch me."

Then I spur my horse for a wild gallop, and my sword and buckler clash against each other.

The fight becomes so fearful, mother, that it would give you a cold shudder could you see it from your palanquin.

Many of them fly, and a great number are cut to pieces.

I know you are thinking, sitting all by yourself, that your boy must be dead by this time.

我喊道："要当心！你们这些坏蛋！再向前走一步，你们就要送命了。"

他们又发出一阵可怕的呐喊声，向前冲过来。

你抓住我的手，说道："好孩子，看在上天面上，躲开他们吧。"

我说道："妈妈，你瞧我的。"

于是我刺策着我的马匹，猛奔过去，我的剑和盾彼此碰着作响。

这一场战斗是那么激烈，妈妈，如果你从轿子里看得见的话，你一定会发冷战的。

他们之中，许多人逃走了，还有好些人被砍杀了。

我知道你那时独自坐在那里，心里正在想着，你的孩子这时候一定已经死了。

But I come to you all stained with blood, and say, "Mother, the fight is over now."

You come out and kiss me, pressing me to your heart, and you say to yourself,

"I don't know what I should do if I hadn't my boy to escort me."

A thousand useless things happen day after day, and why couldn't such a thing come true by chance?

It would be like a story in a book.

My brother would say, "Is it possible? I always thought he was so delicate!"

Our village people would all say in amazement, "Was it not lucky that the boy was with his mother?"

但是我跑到你的跟前，浑身溅满了鲜血，说道："妈妈，现在战争已经结束了。"

你从轿子里走出来，吻着我，把我搂在你的心头，你自言自语地说道：

"如果没有我的孩子护送我，我简直不知道怎么办才好。"

一千件无聊的事天天在发生，为什么这样一件事不能够偶然实现呢？

这很像一本书里的一个故事。

我的哥哥要说道："这是可能的事么？我老是想，他是那么嫩弱呢！"

我们村里的人们都要惊讶地说道："这孩子正和他妈妈在一起，这不是很幸运么？"

The End

It is time for me to go, mother; I am going.

When in the paling darkness of the lonely dawn you stretch out your arms for your baby in the bed, I shall say, "Baby is not there!"—Mother, I am going.

I shall become a delicate draught of air and caress you; and I shall be ripples in the water when you bathe, and kiss you and kiss you again.

In the gusty night when the rain patters on the leaves you will hear my whisper in your bed, and my laughter will flash with the lightning through the open window into your room.

If you lie awake, thinking of your baby till late into the night, I shall sing to you from the stars, "Sleep, mother, sleep."

告 别

是我走的时候了，妈妈，我走了。

当清寂的黎明，你在暗中伸出双臂，要抱你睡在床上的孩子时，我要说道："孩子不在那里呀！"——妈妈，我走了。

我要变成一股清风抚摸着你；我要变成水的涟漪，当你浴时，把你吻了又吻。

大风之夜，当雨点在树叶中淅沥时，你在床上会听见我的微语；当电光从开着的窗口闪进你的屋里时，我的笑声也偕了它一同闪进了。

如果你醒着躺在床上，想你的孩子到深夜，我便要从星空向你唱道："睡呀！妈妈，睡呀。"

新月集 The Crescent Moon

On the straying moonbeams I shall steal over your bed, and lie upon your bosom while you sleep.

I shall become a dream, and through the little opening of your eyelids I shall slip into the depths of your sleep; and when you wake up and look round startled, like a twinkling firefly I shall flit out into the darkness.

When, on the great festival of puja[①], the neighbours' children come and play about the house, I shall melt into the music of the flute and throb in your heart all day.

Dear auntie will come with puja-presents[②] and will ask, "Where is our baby, sister?" Mother, you will tell her softly, "He is in the pupils of my eyes; he is in my body and in my soul."

---

① puja：普耶节。puja 意为"祭神大典"。此处的"普耶节"
  指印度十月间的"难近母祭日"。
② puja-present：普耶礼，指普耶节亲友相互馈赠的礼物。

我要坐在各处游荡的月光上，偷偷地来到你的床上，乘你睡着时，躺在你的胸上。

我要变成一个梦儿，从你眼皮的微缝中，钻到你的睡眠的深处。当你醒来吃惊地四望时，我便如闪耀的萤火似的，熠熠地向暗中飞去了。

当普耶节日，邻舍家的孩子们来屋里游玩时，我便要融化在笛声里，整日价在你心头震荡。

亲爱的阿姨带了普耶礼来，问道："我们的孩子在哪里，姊姊？"妈妈，你将要柔声地告诉她："他呀，他现在是在我的瞳仁里，他现在是在我的身体里，在我的灵魂里。"

The Recall

The night was dark when she went away, and they slept.

The night is dark now, and I call for her, "Come back, my darling; the world is asleep; and no one would know, if you came for a moment while stars are gazing at stars."

She went away when the trees were in bud and the spring was young.

Now the flowers are in high bloom and I call, "Come back, my darling. The children gather and scatter flowers in reckless sport. And if you come and take one little blossom no one will miss it."

Those that used to play are playing still, so spendthrift is life.

召　唤

她走的时候，夜间黑漆漆的，他们都睡了。

现在，夜间也是黑漆漆的，我唤她道："回来，我的宝贝；世界都在沉睡；当星星互相凝视的时候，你来一会儿是没有人知道的。"

她走的时候，树木正在萌芽，春光刚刚来到。

现在花已盛开，我唤道："回来，我的宝贝。孩子们漫不经心地在游戏，把花聚在一起，又把它们散开。你如走来，拿一朵小花去，没有人会发觉的。"

那些常常在游戏的人，仍然还在那里游戏，生命总是如此地浪费。

I listen to their chatter and call, "Come back, my darling, for mother's heart is full to the brim with love, and if you come to snatch only one little kiss from her no one will grudge it."

　　我静听他们的空谈，便唤道："回来，我的宝贝，妈妈的心里充满着爱，你如走来，仅仅从她那里接一个小小的吻，没有人会妒忌的。"

The First Jasmines

Ah, these jasmines, these white jasmines!

I seem to remember the first day when I filled my hands with these jasmines, these white jasmines.

I have loved the sunlight, the sky and the green earth;

I have heard the liquid murmur of the river through the darkness of midnight;

Autumn sunsets have come to me at the bend of a road in the lonely waste, like a bride raising her veil to accept her lover.

Yet my memory is still sweet with the first white jasmines that I held in my hand when I was a child.

第一次的茉莉

呵，这些茉莉花，这些白的茉莉花！

我仿佛记得我第一次双手满捧着这些茉莉花，这些白的茉莉花的时候。

我喜爱那日光，那天空，那绿色的大地；

我听见那河水淙淙的流声，在黑漆的午夜里传过来；

秋天的夕阳，在荒原上大路转角处迎我，如新妇揭起她的面纱迎接她的爱人。

但我想起孩提时第一次捧在手里的白茉莉，心里充满着甜蜜的回忆。

Many a glad day has come in my life, and I have laughed with merrymakers on festival nights.

On grey mornings of rain I have crooned many an idle song.

I have worn round my neck the evening wreath of bakulas woven by the hand of love.

Yet my heart is sweet with the memory of the first fresh jasmines that filled my hands when I was a child.

　　我生平有过许多快活的日子。在节日宴会的晚上，我曾跟着说笑话的人大笑。

　　在灰暗的雨天的早晨，我吟哦过许多飘逸的诗篇。

　　我颈上戴过爱人手织的醉花的花圈，作为晚装。

　　但我想起孩提时第一次捧在手里的白茉莉，心里充满着甜蜜的回忆。

The Banyan Tree

O you shaggy-headed banyan tree standing on the bank of the pond, have you forgotten the little child, like the birds that have nested in your branches and left you?

Do you not remember how he sat at the window and wondered at the tangle of your roots that plunged underground?

The women would come to fill their jars in the pond, and your huge black shadow would wriggle on the water like sleep struggling to wake up.

Sunlight danced on the ripples like restless tiny shuttles weaving golden tapestry.

Two ducks swam by the weedy margin above their shadows, and the child would sit still and think.

榕 树

　　喂，你站在池边的蓬头的榕树，你可曾忘记了那小小的孩子，就像那在你的枝上筑巢又离开了你的鸟儿似的孩子？

　　你不记得他是怎样坐在窗内，诧异地望着你深入地下的纠缠的树根么？

　　妇人们常到池边，汲了满罐的水去。你的大黑影便在水面上摇动，好像睡着的人挣扎着要醒来似的。

　　日光在微波上跳舞，好像不停不息的小梭在织着金色的花毡。

　　两只鸭子挨着芦苇，在芦苇影子上游来游去，孩子静静地坐在那里想着。

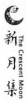

He longed to be the wind and blow through your rustling branches, to be your shadow and lengthen with the day on the water, to be a bird and perch on your top-most twig, and to float like those ducks among the weeds and shadows.

　　他想做风，吹过你的萧萧的枝杈；想做你的影子，在水面上，随着日光而俱长；想做一只鸟儿，栖息在你的最高枝上；还想做那两只鸭，在芦苇与阴影中间游来游去。

Benediction

Bless this little heart, this white soul that has won the kiss of heaven for our earth.

He loves the light of the sun; he loves the sight of his mother's face.

He has not learned to despise the dust, and to hanker after gold.

Clasp him to your heart and bless him.

He has come into this land of a hundred cross-roads.

I know not how he chose you from the crowd, came to your door, and grasped your hand to ask his way.

He will follow you, laughing and talking, and not a doubt in his heart.

祝 福

祝福这个小心灵，这个洁白的灵魂，他为我们的大地，赢得了天的接吻。

他爱日光，他爱见他妈妈的脸。

他没有学会厌恶尘土而渴求黄金。

紧紧把他抱在你心里，并且祝福他。

他已来到这个歧路百出的大地上了。

我不知道他怎么从群众中选出你来，来到你的门前，抓住你的手问路。

他笑着，谈着，跟着你走，心里没有一点儿疑惑。

Keep his trust, lead him straight and bless him.

Lay your hand on his head, and pray that though the waves underneath grow threatening, yet the breath from above may come and fill his sails and waft him to the haven of peace.

Forget him not in your hurry, let him come to your heart and bless him.

不要辜负他的信任，引导他到正路，并且祝福他。

把你的手按在他的头上，祈求着：底下的波涛虽然险恶，然而从上面来的风会鼓起他的船帆，送他到和平的港口的。

不要在忙碌中把他忘了，让他来到你的心里，并且祝福他。

The Gift

I want to give you something, my child, for we are drifting in the stream of the world.

Our lives will be carried apart, and our love forgotten.

But I am not so foolish as to hope that I could buy your heart with my gifts.

Young is your life, your path long, and you drink the love we bring you at one draught and turn and run away from us.

You have your play and your playmates. What harm is there if you have no time or thought for us?

We, indeed, have leisure enough in old age to count the days that are past, to cherish in our hearts what our hands have lost for ever.

The river runs swift with a song, breaking through all barriers. But the mountain stays and remembers, and follows her with his love.

赠 品

我要送些东西给你，我的孩子，因为我们同是漂泊在世界的溪流中的。

我们的生命将被分开，我们的爱也将被忘记。

但我却没有那样傻，希望能用我的赠品来买你的心。

你的生命正是青青，你的道路也长着呢，你一口气饮尽了我们带给你的爱，便回身离开我们跑了。

你有你的游戏，有你的游伴。如果你没有时间同我们在一起，如果你想不到我们，那有什么害处呢?

我们呢，自然地，在老年时，会有许多闲暇的时间，去计算那过去的日子，把我们手里永久丢失了的东西，在心里爱抚着。

河流唱着歌很快地流去，冲破所有的堤防。但是山峰却留在那里，忆念着，满怀依依之情。

My Song

This song of mine will wind its music around you, my child, like the fond arms of love.

This song of mine will touch your forehead like a kiss of blessing.

When you are alone it will sit by your side and whisper in your ear; when you are in the crowd it will fence you about with aloofness.

My song will be like a pair of wings to your dreams; it will transport your heart to the verge of the unknown.

It will be like the faithful star overhead when dark night is over your road.

My song will sit in the pupils of your eyes, and will carry your sight into the heart of things.

And when my voice is silent in death, my song will speak in your living heart.

我 的 歌

我的孩子，我这一支歌将用它的乐声围绕你，好像那爱情的热恋的手臂一样。

我这一支歌将触着你的前额，好像那祝福的接吻一样。

当你只是一个人的时候，它将坐在你的身旁，在你耳边微语着；当你在人群中的时候，它将围住你，使你超然物外。

我的歌将成为你的梦的翼翅，它将把你的心移送到不可知的岸边。

当黑夜覆盖在你路上的时候，它又将成为那照临在你头上的忠实的星光。

我的歌又将坐在你眼睛的瞳仁里，将你的视线带入万物的心里。

当我的声音因死亡而沉寂时，我的歌仍将在你活泼泼的心中唱着。

The Child-Angel

They clamour and fight, they doubt and despair, they know no end to their wranglings.

Let your life come amongst them like a flame of light, my child, unflickering and pure, and delight them into silence.

They are cruel in their greed and their envy, their words are like hidden knives thirsting for blood.

Go and stand amidst their scowling hearts, my child, and let your gentle eyes fall upon them like the forgiving peace of the evening over the strife of the day.

Let them see your face, my child, and thus know the meaning of all things; let them love you and thus love each other.

孩子天使

他们喧哗争斗，他们怀疑失望，他们辩论而没有结果。

我的孩子，让你的生命到他们当中去，如一线镇定而纯洁之光，使他们愉悦而沉默。

他们的贪心和妒忌是残忍的；他们的话，好像暗藏的刀，渴欲饮血。

我的孩子，去，去站在他们愤懑的心中，把你的和善的眼光落在他们上面，好像那傍晚的宽宏大量的和平，覆盖着日间的骚扰一样。

我的孩子，让他们望着你的脸，因此能够知道一切事物的意义；让他们爱你，因此他们能够相爱。

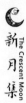

Come and take your seat in the bosom of the limitless, my child. At sunrise open and raise your heart like a blossoming flower, and at sunset bend your head and in silence complete the worship of the day.

　　来，坐在无垠的胸膛上，我的孩子。在朝阳出来时，开放而且抬起你的心，像一朵盛开的花；在夕阳落下时，低下你的头，默默地做完这一天的礼拜。

The Last Bargain

"Come and hire me," I cried, while in the morning I was walking on the stone-paved road.

Sword in hand, the King came in his chariot.

He held my hand and said, "I will hire you with my power."

But his power counted for nought, and he went away in his chariot.

In the heat of the midday the houses stood with shut doors.

I wandered along the crooked lane.

An old man came out with his bag of gold.

He pondered and said, "I will hire you with my money."

最后的买卖

早晨，我在石铺的路上走时，我叫道："谁来雇用我呀。"

皇帝坐着马车，手里拿着剑走来。

他拉着我的手，说道："我要用权力来雇用你。"

但是他的权力算不了什么，他坐着马车走了。

正午炎热的时候，家家户户的门都闭着。

我沿着屈曲的小巷走去。

一个老人带着一袋金钱走出来。

他斟酌了一下，说道："我要用金钱来雇用你。"

He weighed his coins one by one, but I turned away.

It was evening. The garden hedge was all aflower.

The fair maid came out and said, "I will hire you with a smile."

Her smile paled and melted into tears, and she went back alone into the dark.

The sun glistened on the sand, and the sea waves broke waywardly.

A child sat playing with shells.

He raised his head and seemed to know me, and said, "I hire you with nothing."

From thenceforward that bargain struck in child's play made me a free man.

他一个一个地数着他的钱，但我却转身离去了。

黄昏了，花园的篱上满开着花。

美人走出来，说道："我要用微笑来雇用你。"

她的微笑黯淡了，化成泪容了，她孤寂地回身走进黑暗里去。

太阳照耀在沙地上，海波任性地浪花四溅。

一个小孩坐在那里玩贝壳。

他抬起头来，好像认识我似的，说道："我雇你不用什么东西。"

从此以后，在这个小孩的游戏中做成的买卖，使我成了一个自由的人。